ECOLOGY ALERT!

Transportation

Andrew and Amanda Church

RAINTREE
STECK-VAUGHN
PUBLISHERS
A Steck-Vaughn Company

Austin, Texas

Ecology Alert!

Coasts
Energy
Farming

Communities
Transportation
Rivers

Cover: Air traffic controllers look out over a busy airport.
Title page: A highway interchange
Contents page: A bicycle parking lot in China

Published by Raintree Steck-Vaughn Publishers, an imprint of Steck-Vaughn Company

Library of Congress Cataloging-in-Publication Data
Church, Andrew and Amanda.
Transportation / Andrew and Amanda Church.
    p.   cm.—(Ecology Alert)
Includes bibliographical references and index.
Summary: Describes different modes of transportation developed in different areas of the world with special emphasis on their environmental consequences.
ISBN 0-8172-5372-6
1. Transportation—Juvenile literature.
2. Transportation—Environmental aspects—Juvenile literature.
[1. Transportation. 2. Pollution.]
I. Church, Amanda. II. Title. III. Series.
HE152.C69 1999
388—dc21   98-34741

Printed in Italy. Bound in the United States.
1 2 3 4 5 6 7 8 9 0 03 02 01 00 99

Picture acknowledgments
Axiom Photographic Agency (Steve Benbow) 23, (Steve Benbow) 25, (Jim Holmes) 26; James Davis Travel Photography 20; Ecoscene (Melanie Peters) 8, 13, (John Farmar) 28; Eye Ubiquitous (Julia Bayne) 7; (J. C. Pasieka) 21; Foster and Partners 29 both; Impact Photos (Charles Coates) 4, (Christophe Bluntzer) 6, (Trevor Morgan) 12, (Alain Evrard) 24; Tony Stone Images (Paul Chesley) cover, (Baron Wolman) 1, (Don Smetzer) 10, (Richard Brown) 11, (David Woodfall) 14, (Will & Deni McIntyre) 15, (George Hunter) 22; Wayland Picture Library (Julia Waterlow) 3, 5, 16, 18, (A. Blackburn) 19.

Artwork by Peter Bull Art Studio.

Contents

Moving Around

A father carries his baby in a sling to do the shopping. The baby sleeps and is content. What neither of them realizes is that they are using probably one of the first means of transportation discovered by humans. For early humans, walking was the only way to get around. Nowadays, there are hundreds of different types of vehicles that move people and goods around the world, ranging from bicycles to airplanes and from canoes to tankers.

All forms of transportation use energy to make things move. Walking uses our body's energy that comes from food. A car uses gasoline as a source of energy.

A busy street in India is filled with many different means of transportation.

Some sources of energy use up natural resources, such as oil, that will eventually run out. Other types of energy will last forever. Wind power moves sailing ships, and power from the sun may drive cars in the future. The wind and the sun are sources of energy that will not run out.

All forms of transportation can have a bad effect on our environment, whatever the energy source. For example, we all know that cars create air pollution. Although walking has very little impact, too many hikers in one place can destroy trails and damage areas of natural beauty.

We need transportation for many purposes, such as for going to school, taking vacations, shopping, and going to work.

Moving around is essential to our lives, but in the future we will have to find forms of transportation that cause less harm to the environment. We may also be forced to move around less.

The development of transportation
Until 200 years ago, the main forms of transportation and sources of energy were:
- **Walking using human energy.**
- **Wind-powered sailing ships on the sea.**
- **Carts and carriages using energy from horses.**

In the nineteenth and twentieth centuries a range of inventions changed travel forever.

1769–1813	**Steamboats and trains developed.**
1783	**Air transportation began with the first hot-air balloon.**
1880s	**The internal combustion engine was used in motorized vehicles.**
1900–1910	**First airplanes.**
1961	**Yuri Gagarin was the first person to travel in space.**

The skateboard above, roller blades, ice skates, skis, and surfboards are all forms of transportation.

Did you jump in the car to get to school today? Could you have walked instead? Walking to school would have used less energy and caused less harm to the environment.

Local Travel Using Body Energy

The most common trips people take are in their local areas, near where they live. These trips are quite short. They might be trips to school, to work, to the store, or to see friends and relatives. Many of these trips can be made by walking or bicycling using energy made by our bodies. The food we eat is digested, and our blood and muscles turn it into energy, which allows us to move.

Animals as transportation

Horse-drawn carts in Romania. Animals are a slow means of transportation.

In a similar way, the body energy of animals can be used to transport people and goods. In many farming areas of the world, animals such as horses, oxen, bullocks, yaks, and even dogs are used to pull heavy loads.

Bicycles

Bicycling is a good way to use body energy for transportation. The pedals and chain transfer energy from people's legs to the wheels. Using the same amount of energy, bicycles allow us to travel farther and faster than we could if we walked.

There are about 850 million bicycles in the world. Bicycles are not harmful to the environment, because they cause little or no pollution. They are good for you as well: cycling is an excellent form of exercise.

Bike-only routes make it safe and easy to move around a local area.

However, many people avoid using bicycles because they feel roads are too dangerous. Some cities are trying to make it easier and safer for people to bicycle. In Odense, in Denmark, special bike-only routes have made cycling safer, and six out of ten children bicycle to school.

Finding what we need locally

Using local stores is less harmful to our environment than traveling to stores some distance away. By traveling shorter distances, we use less energy and create less pollution.

In poorer countries, outside big cities, people often have no choice. They cannot afford forms of transportation other than walking, so they walk to buy or collect what they need. For example, in many developing countries, people spend over three hours each day collecting the wood that is their only source of fuel.

Using energy

Different forms of transportation use up different amounts of energy. Energy use is measured in megajoules. This table shows you how much energy different means of transportation use for traveling around a town.

TYPE OF TRANSPORTATION	MEGAJOULES OF ENERGY PER PERSON PER MI. (KM)
Large car	6.77 (4.23)
Motorcycle	4.27 (2.67)
Small car	3.87 (2.42)
Bus (half full)	0.99 (0.62)
Train (two-thirds full)	0.90 (0.56)
Walking	0.40 (0.25)
Bicycling	0.09 (0.06)

In richer countries, most of us have a choice about how we travel around our local area. We can walk, bicycle, take a bus, or drive. Too often we use a car to make a short trip without even thinking of other ways of traveling. In the United Kingdom, for example, 70 percent of car trips are under 5 mi. (8 km), a distance that many people could bicycle.

In richer countries, many people use their cars all the time, even when there are other forms of transportation.

A new transportation system

A new form of public transportation is being developed in Amsterdam, the largest city in the Netherlands.

The idea for the "White Bike System" was first used in Amsterdam in the 1960s. Large numbers of bicycles were painted white to make them look different from private bicycles. If someone needed to go somewhere they used a white bicycle and then left it on the street at their destination for another person to use. However, all the bicycles eventually disappeared, and the system did not work anymore.

Now this idea has been updated using a computer system to control renting bicycles around the city. The person who wants to rent the bike uses a special "smart" card (like a credit card) to reserve the bike, pay, and claim a parking space at his or her destination. The computer also prints out a route of where the person wants to go.

The system is still being developed, so it cannot be used in many places yet. However, it aims to improve public transportation and make it easier for people to move around the city.

Cyclists using the computer to rent "white bikes" in Amsterdam

Food and transportation

In cities all over the world, many people drive to out-of-town shopping centers to buy food rather than go to the nearest store. Often the food they buy has been shipped a long way to get to these shopping centers. Next time you buy an apple, find out where it came from. It may have been transported from New Zealand or Canada by plane or boat.

In the United States, many cities now have farmers' markets. The food on sale is grown in the local area and has been transported only a short distance. This uses less energy and thus causes less pollution.

Transportation for all

Walking and bicycling are easier for some people than for others. In Europe, for example, one out of ten people have difficulty walking up steps. These are mainly older or disabled people. Many of these people can walk only if sidewalks do not have too many obstacles, such as cracks and steps. Too many steps and rough sidewalks are also difficult for very young children and for parents pushing children in strollers or baby carriages.

Streets and sidewalks should be designed so they can be used by everyone. This must include people who have problems walking and people who are disabled.

Activity

School transportation survey

Working in a group, draw up a list of questions to ask the whole class. You are trying to find out:

- How they travel to and from school.
- How long it takes them.
- How far they travel.

In the United States, many children take school buses to get to school.

Make sure you use words that are clear and will get you the information you want. Discuss with the teacher the lists each group has made and agree on a set of questions that should be completed by the whole class.

Ask each pupil to complete the survey at home. Some may need help to figure out how far they travel and how long it takes.

Use this information to create pictorial graphs of the trip to school of pupils in the class.

Figure out roughly how much energy each pupil uses to get to school, using the fact box on page 8. Write down ways you think pupils could change the way they travel to school so that they use less energy.

Travel Using Energy from the Environment

Methods of transportation, such as buses, trains, and streetcars, allow people to travel more quickly around local areas. The environment provides the energy for these vehicles. The energy sources include oil and coal, which are burned, and energy in the form of electricity.

Fossil fuels

Coal, oil, and natural gas are called fossil fuels. They were formed under the earth's surface by the remains of plants and animals that died millions of years ago. Gasoline and diesel fuel are made from oil. Fossil fuels are not limitless, and the quicker we use them the sooner they will run out.

Cars and buses

Cars and buses use gasoline or diesel fuel for energy. Both come from oil. Burning oil causes serious pollution.

Trains and streetcars

Different types of trains may be used for local travel. In some countries, older trains run on diesel fuel or coal. Buses, trains, and streetcars are known as public transportation, because anyone can travel on them.

This streetcar in Melbourne, Australia, runs on electricity from overhead wires.

The impact of an electric train or streetcar on the environment will depend on how the electricity has been made. If it comes from a power plant making electricity by burning coal, oil, or gas, it will create pollution and use up fuel. If the power plant uses wind or water as the source of energy, then it will create far less pollution and will not use up fuels that cannot be replaced.

In many countries people are using cars, even when buses, trains, or streetcars are available.

Why do people prefer to drive?

Cars allow people to make many short trips one after another. Cars take people right where they want to go. In bad weather a car provides shelter. For disabled people, cars may be the only way they can travel easily. Many people feel safer from crime traveling by car compared with using public transportation. In some areas, especially in the remote countryside, people use cars because there are not enough buses and trains.

The number of cars in the world will increase from about 600 million now to 750 million by 2005. Many people who do not own a car would like to buy one.

Pollution from cars

Two of the gases from car exhaust are nitrogen oxide and hydrocarbons.

On sunny days they mix with sunlight to form smog, which makes it hard for some people to breathe.

Nitrogen oxide mixes with water in the clouds to make acid rain, which damages buildings and harms plants and wildlife.

The problems caused by cars

Cars are among the biggest causes of air pollution, which can harm people's health.

Cars also produce carbon dioxide, which is one of the greenhouse gases. These gases form a layer around the earth and trap heat near its surface. Without this layer of gases, the earth would be very cold and could not support life.

The gases in car exhausts are bad for people's health and cause air pollution.

However, more and more of these gases are being released into the atmosphere. This is making the earth warmer, and it may change climates all over the world. This could have serious effects for everyone. Food production would be affected, many countries would be flooded, serious diseases might spread, and some plants and animals would die out.

In some countries people are so worried about air pollution from cars that new laws have been passed. Car companies are being forced to make cars with very few polluting gases in their exhaust.

People imagine the car to be the quickest form of transportation for short trips, but in cities the roads are often so clogged by traffic that travel by car takes longer than it should. Cars have made some roads very busy, especially in the rush hour at the beginning and end of a working day.

Traffic jams make road travel slower. They also increase the pollution caused by cars.

Activity

Investigate traffic flow

Working in small groups, choose a busy road near your school to investigate traffic. Be sure to have an adult with you. Count how many cars, trucks, vans, and bicycles go by in a 15-minute period. Make a table to present this information. Back in the classroom, draw a graph to display the results.

How many people are there in each vehicle during the same 15-minute period? Figure out a way of displaying this information. Could people share cars? How would this change the number of cars on the road?

What is the most common vehicle? Do most cars have a driver and no passengers? Consider the alternative forms of transportation in your area. Could the road be made safer for pedestrians and bicycles?

All these problems caused by the car affect everyone in a country. This is unfair to people who do not have cars. They get all the problems of cars without having the benefits of owning one.

What can we use instead of the car?

Moving a large number of people by bus or train uses much less energy than if the same number of people all used cars. Using public transportation, such as buses, streetcars, or trains, is better for the environment than using cars. Public transportation reduces the number of cars on the roads.

A train in Argentina. Trains can move a large number of people very efficiently.

To encourage people to use public transportation, it must be safe and not too expensive; it must stop near people's homes, arrive on time, and be pleasant to use. The problem is that good public transportation costs money. But so does building roads for cars and cleaning up their pollution.

CASE STUDY

Using cars

Mark and Beth Maloney live with their four children in Luray, Virginia, a small town about two and a half hours from Washington, D.C.

Mark works as a manager in a factory. To get to work, he has to drive 30 mi. (48 km). He uses the family's small car. He says there is no alternative to using a car: "There are no local buses, and I don't even know where the nearest railroad station is."

Beth is a registered nurse at the local hospital. Although her trip is only a mile (1.6 km), she drives the family's other car, a four-door sedan. "I could bike to work, but I have to drop Thomas, who is three, off at the baby-sitter's first. To be honest, I just wouldn't feel safe coming home on a bike late at night. A car is much more convenient." The other three children get themselves to school by walking five minutes.

Mark explained that there is no public transportation around their local area. "There are no local buses, and the nearest Greyhound bus terminal is 20 mi. [32 km] away. Everyone we know around here has a car, and most people have two."

There is no public transportation where the Maloneys live, so they use their cars all the time.

17

Long-distance Travel

Many of the trips that take people and goods outside their local areas are made for business reasons. Some trips are made by car, but over long distances, trains and airplanes can be much quicker.

Some companies are trying to reduce the time their staff spends traveling by using video links for meetings. That way, people in different places—even on other sides of the world—can see each other talking without having to travel.

Freight

Goods are moved around a country by truck, train, airplane, or boat. The chosen means of transportation depends on cost, speed, and the size of the load.

- Boats on big rivers, such as the Mississippi, can move heavy loads cheaply, but they are slow.
- Train and truck transportation is quicker but often more expensive. Many businesses prefer to use trucks because goods can go directly to their destination, which saves time and money.
- It is expensive to transport goods by air, and planes are mostly used to move something quickly that is valuable and does not weigh very much.

Ships on the Rhine in Germany. Around the world, many rivers are major transportation routes.

Environmental impact

For moving goods, boats tend to cause the least damage to the environment because they use the smallest amount of energy for each ton of goods.

Planes move many people quickly, but jet engine fuel creates harmful gases.

Trucks probably do the most environmental harm because they create pollution from their exhausts, damage roads, and shake buildings. Trucks use a lot more energy for each ton of goods compared with trains or boats, because each truck carries only a small load.

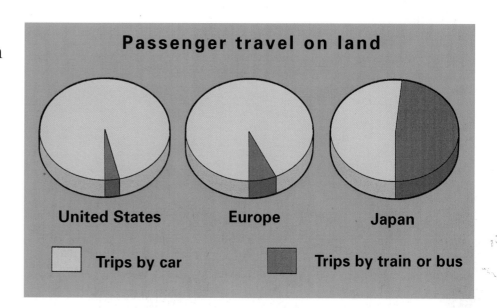

Passenger travel on land

United States   Europe   Japan

Trips by car   Trips by train or bus

Activity

Measuring congestion

People and goods need to get to their destinations on time. If roads or highways are crowded, traffic will be slowed down.

Each road or route has a capacity. This is the number of vehicles it can carry safely and at a reasonable speed. Congestion occurs when there are more vehicles than the route can carry.

You can do this exercise in school or in a large room. You will need a stopwatch, two chairs, and the whole class.

1 Line up the chairs about 6 ft. (2 m) apart and line up the class in pairs.

2 The pairs then move between the chairs as quickly as possible without bumping into each other. Time how long it takes.

3 Then try it in groups of threes and fours. The capacity of the "road" between the chairs is reached when the number of children trying to move through at the same time start bumping into each other and congestion occurs. What is the capacity of the "road"?

4 Repeat the experiment with a 3-ft. (1-m) or a 10-ft. (3 m) space between the chairs.

Imagine that the space between the chairs is a door and your class has to go through it in an emergency. Have a discussion about the safest way to leave your classroom in an emergency.

A crowded street in Delhi, India. Congestion happens where there are too many people or vehicles for the space available.

In some countries, travel beyond the local area is difficult. Their governments do not have much money, so roads and railroads are not very good or do not exist at all. In these countries, transportation by river and air are often the only reliable way to travel long distances.

CASE STUDY

Travel in Gabon

Jean Ivombo lives with his wife, Eugenie, and their three children in Gamba, a small town in Gabon, West Africa. He works for Shell Gabon at an oil terminal on the coast.

For their annual vacation, Jean and his family visit Eugenie's parents in the small village of Ndende, deep in the rain forest. It is possible to take a bush taxi, but it takes 10 hours to cover the 236 mi. (380 km) because the roads are often washed away by tropical storms and are very bumpy. Even though it is much more expensive, Jean chooses to fly and then cover the last section of the journey by taxi.

The government in Gabon would like to build better roads but is afraid that this will open up the rain forest areas too much. People may move in and cut down the trees to make land for farming.

Improving road transportation would make life easier for people in Gabon, but the rain forest would be damaged in the process. Rain forests are very important because they contain many rare species of plants and animals. They also help control the earth's climate.

Jean Ivombo and his family like to travel to the rain forest.

Making new roads through forest land destroys the natural landscape.

International Travel

Goods and ships

Goods sent between countries that are oceans apart are usually moved by ship. Goods on a ship are called cargo. Cargo is often packed into containers, which are huge metal boxes that stack on top of each other. Supertankers, which carry oil, are the largest forms of transportation in the world. Some are 1,500 ft. (450 m) long.

International travel is too expensive for most people in the world, but more tourists visit other countries for their vacations than ever before.

Vacation travel

Planes, cars, and fast trains have allowed many people to travel much farther on vacation than they used to 30 years ago. For example, in 1985 about 3 million people from Europe visited the United States. Now it is about 9 million people a year, and nearly all of them travel by plane.

Tourism can have good and bad effects on the places people visit.

The benefits of tourism

Tourism brings money to a country and creates jobs for the people who live there. New stores and roads built for tourists may be useful for local people. Traveling abroad allows people from different countries to meet and perhaps understand each other better.

The problems of tourism

Tourism can destroy the very places people travel to see. For example, ancient Roman and Greek buildings have been damaged by the huge numbers of people walking in them.

Tourists can also harm the environment and wildlife. In the Caribbean, extra waste caused by tourism has poisoned mangrove swamps, and divers have damaged coral reefs.

In poor countries, land, food, water, and fuel may be used for tourists instead of for local people. In places where few people have visited, tourism can change the way of life. Remote tribes of people in South America and Asia also have been infected by diseases that had never been known before tourists brought them into the area.

Popular vacation spots such as resorts in Florida and Spain (above) have been spoiled by too many large hotels and pollution.

Tourism in the Mediterranean

- Each year, more than 160 million people visit the coastal areas and islands of the Mediterranean Sea.
- Three-fourths of the sand dunes between Gibraltar in Spain and Sicily in Italy have disappeared because of new buildings.
- Hotel construction in part of Turkey was stopped to save a type of turtle, called the loggerhead turtle. The construction was destroying the turtles' habitat. Now the turtles attract an extra 5,000 tourists a year, creating other environmental problems.

Tourism in Bali

Bali is one of the smallest islands in Indonesia. It lies 8 degrees south of the equator and has a pleasant, warm climate. The island has a population of 3.5 million people. The Balinese people follow the Hindu religion and have many colorful ceremonies and festivals. Painting, dancing, music, puppet-making, and kite-flying are popular pastimes.

As a result of cheap air travel, many hotels have been built in Bali.

The first tourists came to Bali in the 1920s, traveling by ship. European people opened a few hotels in the 1950s and 1960s. When the first beach hotel was opened at Sanur, in 1966, Balinese people came from all over the island to see the running water, electricity, and elevators.

The 1970s brought cheap international air travel, and large numbers of people started to come to Bali. Now more than 350,000 people visit every year, flying in from Europe, the United States, and Australia.

New roads and highways have been built; hotels, stores, restaurants, and nightclubs have opened; markets are open at night, and roads in tourist areas are full of cars and motorcycles. While many Balinese people have made money and improved their standard of living, parts of Bali have changed forever as a result of cheap international air travel.

Tourists visiting another country can try to reduce the harmful effects of tourism, such as pollution. They can choose to visit places where their visit will not damage the environment or change other people's way of life.

A group of tourists in the Galapagos Islands, in South America. They are learning about the islands' unique animals and plants.

Activity

Being a good tourist

Imagine some schoolchildren are going to visit your local area. They come from another country where the way of life is different. They have written to you, wanting to know how to be a good tourist in your area. They want to know:

- The best places to visit in your local area.
- How they should travel around your local area.
- How they should behave in public places and stores.
- What to do if they bump into someone or get in someone's way.
- How they should behave in cafés and restaurants.

Make a postcard to send them. Divide the front into four quarters and in each quarter draw a picture of one of the places you think they should visit. Write on the back, giving answers to their questions.

Travel in the Future

People move around for many reasons, from shopping near their homes to going on vacation on the other side of the world.

Using cars less

The most common form of transportation around the world is the car. Car transportation is a particular problem because it creates pollution, and each car moves very few people. We need to encourage people to use cars less. Some organizations have suggested that governments should:

- Spend more on buses, trains, and streetcars. This would make public transportation a good alternative to cars, especially for long trips.
- Encourage people who drive to work to share cars.
- Build safe routes to school so children can walk and bicycle.
- Keep companies from building out-of-town shopping centers, because most people have to drive to them.
- Make driving more expensive by raising the price of gasoline and parking.
- Make more city areas car free, so they are pleasant for pedestrians and bicyclists.

It is difficult for children to walk to school if there are no sidewalks.

Less damage to the environment

The car is not the only problem. All transportation uses energy and has some impact on the environment.

To reduce environmental damage, we need to change how we live, and we must move around less. We could do this by:

- Working from home, using computers, modems, and faxes. In the United States, nearly 4 million people now work from home.
- Shopping from home by computer, ordering goods that are then delivered to people's homes.
- Encouraging people to use local stores and to buy food that is grown locally.
- Building new houses near city centers and places where there are jobs, so people do not have to travel so far to get to work.

A covered market in Portugal. Buying food that has been made or grown locally uses less energy.

In the future there will be many new forms of transportation, on land, on the sea, and in the air.

Some amazing inventions will allow the richer people in the world to travel farther and faster, using less energy and creating less pollution. New types of supersonic airplanes that will be quieter, bigger, and quicker than the Concorde are being planned. Cars that use energy from the sun have already been made, and they may be developed further for countries that have plenty of sun.

But not everyone in the world will benefit from these changes. We also need to develop transportation that poorer people can use to make their lives easier and more pleasant.

A few solar-powered cars have been built by big car companies. This car attracts interest in a street in Australia.